Summary

of

Johann Hari's

Lost Connections

Uncovering the Real Causes of Depression — and the Unexpected Solutions

by
Swift Reads

.

Table of Contents

Overview

Lost Connections: Uncovering the Real Causes of Depression — and the Unexpected Solutions (2018) explores the physical, psychological, and cultural factors that lead to depression, as well as the tactics communities can employ to overcome it. British journalist Johann Hari argues that while depression can have a biological cause, it's largely an involuntary reaction to the social ills that plague modern society. Antidepressants, while widely advertised as a solution for depression, often only serve to mask the problem if patients are not encouraged to confront what is making them unhappy. If medical institutions and governments address the underlying causes of distress in society, they can reduce the rate of depression and promote better social cohesion.

Before the 1970s, researchers grouped depressed patients into those whose sadness stemmed from a biologically based mental disorder and those whose depression was sparked by experiencing negative events. An anthropologist named George Brown decided to test the theory of biological cause by interviewing women in South London who had been diagnosed with depression. Brown and his associate, therapist Tirril Harris, discovered that most of the women diagnosed with depression had gone through one or more stressful life events shortly before they were diagnosed. Their findings held true regardless of whether the women's doctors attributed their depression to biological causes or personal history.

In the 1990s, a number of doctors continued to seek a purely biological explanation for depression. The most popular theory was that depressed patients suffered from depleted levels of serotonin, a chemical in the brain usually connected to happiness. Antidepressants became seen as a way to correct this chemical imbalance and return the patient to normal functioning. Pharmaceutical companies began marketing dozens of antidepressants, all of which supposedly provided greater benefit than placebos.

As antidepressants became more popular in the 1990s, a Harvard Medical School professor named Irving Kirsch challenged the widespread treatment method by examining the scientific studies that supported the pharmaceutical companies' claims. He discovered that only a quarter of the drugs' effects could be attributed to the pills; the rest could either be chalked up to the placebo effect, or to the human brain's ability to recover from depression over time. Moreover, Kirsch learned that most scientists who studied depression no longer used low serotonin levels to explain the disorder. Researchers didn't know what brain chemical, if any, caused depression; drugs that artificially suppressed serotonin didn't seem to cause depression any more than drugs that provided serotonin boosts seemed to cure it.

Kirsch's findings contradicted the studies published by pharmaceutical companies, which used a small amount of research to bolster their claims. Drug regulators only require that companies produce a couple of trials showing that their drug works; even if the drug fails to produce the desired effect in the majority of pre-market testing, it can still be sold if at least two trials are successful. The idea that depression and anxiety are caused primarily by a chemical imbalance is not supported by scientific evidence, but was promoted to the public because it allowed drug companies to make money. The explanation was additionally easy to swallow because it allowed sufferers to simply take pills, rather than examine the source of their unhappiness.

In the decades since researchers like Brown and Harris started studying depression, scientists have identified nine social and mental factors that can lead to the mood disorder. Those causes include diminished access to meaningful jobs, social isolation, lack of higher purpose, and childhood trauma. Being treated as an inferior, not spending time in nature, inability to assure future security, and in some rare cases, biological predispositions, can additionally cause depression. Both anxiety and depression can be mitigated or even cured, however, when a person is offered a remedy, such as the chance to form bonds with others or pursue personal dreams. If governments and doctors can recognize depression as a social ill, rather than an individual mental disorder, then leaders can begin to build communities that meet everyone's basic needs, thereby eliminating many of the outward forces that cause depression and anxiety.

Key Insights

1. The placebo effect can be observed whenever anyone takes any kind of medication.

2. Depression and anxiety do not typically stem from neurological causes; however, depression can still be reinforced neurologically if maladaptive thoughts and behaviors become habitual.

3. Demeaning or unsatisfying jobs can lead to depression, especially if an employee feels trapped in a profession.

4. Humans have become increasingly socially isolated, which has led to increased rates of loneliness.

5. Material possessions and personal accolades may provide a temporary mood boost, but won't lead to lasting happiness.

6. Spending time in nature can decrease depression and anxiety.

7. To decrease depression, sufferers must focus on something greater than themselves.

8. If a community reduces social inequality and poverty, the rates of depression and anxiety will also decrease.

Key Insight 1

The placebo effect can be observed whenever anyone takes any kind of medication.

Analysis

In the 1700s, a British doctor named John Haygarth realized that patients could be cured, at least temporarily, of their ailments if they believed in the doctor's recommended treatment. The phenomenon, known as the placebo effect, still plays a role in modern medicine. A patient's belief in a medication's effectiveness determines, at least in part, whether it will work as expected. Since the placebo effect is always present in medical treatment, scientists and doctors have to tease out how much of a medication's effects are due to the placebo effect rather than the actual treatment.

Even if a placebo does not contain any medication, it can still help patients find relief from ailments. In a 2018 BBC article, journalist Michael Mosley explains the results of a placebo experiment conducted as part of the BBC2 Horizon television show *Can My Brain Cure My Body?* (2018). During the experiment, 100 people who suffered from back pain took part in a drug trial in which they were told they would be given either a placebo or a new pain medication. Unbeknownst to the participants, everyone received a pill that contained only rice. For about 50 of the participants, the pills worked. They no longer felt back pain, and no longer had to turn to addictive painkillers. A University of Oxford professor, Irene Tracey, told BBC that one reason placebos create a real and measurable effect on the human body is because they encourage the release of endorphins and other physical chemicals that relieve pain naturally. The BBC experiment suggests that it may be beneficial in some cases for doctors to prescribe placebos to their patients to alleviate pain or other long-standing ailments.

Key Insight 2

Depression and anxiety do not typically stem from neurological causes; however, depression can still be reinforced neurologically if maladaptive thoughts and behaviors become habitual.

Analysis

Human brains have a tendency to replicate and reinforce the same patterns over and over, especially if those patterns were once used for self-preservation. For example, if an abused woman became fearful of others during her ordeal, her brain may encourage her to stay distant and antisocial long after the danger has passed. These thought patterns can be difficult to break; however, the brain is malleable and adaptive. If depressed people are taught psychological strategies that help to fight old habits, they can form new thought patterns that reformat the brain toward health and happiness.

In the 2000s and 2010s, researchers have studied whether psychedelics can help depressed people break out of old, maladaptive thought patterns. In his book *How to Change Your Mind: What the New Science of Psychedelics Teaches Us About*

Consciousness, Dying, Addiction, Depression, and Transcendence (2018), journalist Michael Pollan explains that some researchers believe psychedelic drugs might quiet a section of the brain known as the default mode network. That part of the brain is responsible for reflective thought and analysis, such as remembering the past or worrying about a friend. It also appears during self-reflection or anxious pondering of the future. Researchers believe that the default mode network becomes overactive in people who suffer from depression. This traps the brain into circular modes of thought so that a depressed person has a hard time breaking away from self-reflection and rumination. By temporarily deactivating the default mode network, psychedelic drugs might allow a depressed person to come to new realizations and to reexamine old thought patterns from a new perspective. Researchers are still exploring the default mode network, and hope to learn more about how it functions in brains that exhibit no mood disorders or mental illnesses. With more time, scientists may be able to further manipulate that section of the brain so that doctors can better treat patients with depression.

Key Insight 3

Demeaning or unsatisfying jobs can lead to depression, especially if an employee feels trapped in a profession.

Analysis

In the early 2010s, polling company Gallup studied workplace satisfaction in more than 140 countries. The company found that over half of employees are dispassionate about their jobs. Nearly a quarter are so unhappy that they actively want to sabotage both their employers and their teammates. If workers feel trapped in jobs that they hate, they are likely to become depressed and unproductive at best, and actively antagonistic at worst.

In some cases, workers may become unhappy not because they don't value their profession, but because their company has created a hostile work environment. In 2018, hundreds of Google employees went on strike to protest the company's policies for handling worker complaints including sexual harassment. Google required all employees to sign a contract agreeing to report harassment to company officials and go through an internal arbitration process. Workers were not allowed to pursue a civil court case against the company.

Though Google quickly agreed to reforms, such policies remain in effect in other companies, ensuring that those who endure sexual harassment are at the mercy of their higher-ups, who may or may not be the perpetrators. The arbitration process is fully in the company's favor.

According to the Economic Policy Institute, a think tank based in Washington, DC, more than half of private companies without a union enforce an internal arbitration process. That mandatory arbitration process leaves millions of workers in the United States with no way to take their employers to court if they discover that their rights aren't being met at work. If employees work at such a company and realize that they have no way of ensuring that harassers will be brought to justice, they naturally may grow depressed. Protecting the ability of workers to access the courts not only can decrease rates of depression in the workforce, but also can improve productivity, which can help the economy.

Key Insight 4

Humans have become increasingly socially isolated, which has led to increased rates of loneliness.

Analysis

Humans evolved to be social creatures, but as society has developed new technologies, humans have increasingly been able to survive without staying in close proximity with each other. Nevertheless, most people still crave human contact, and will become lonely if they isolate themselves from others. Although internet venues like social media or online gaming can provide some connection with other people, it still doesn't satisfy innate human needs in the way that in-person social communion would.

Social isolation has additionally led to an increase in the number of people who never or rarely experience physical contact. According to a 2018 *Guardian* article, scientists have shown that being touched provides numerous physical and mental benefits, such as lowering heart rate and blood pressure, decreasing stress, and boosting the immune system. Gentle touch can improve social bonds and leave people feeling less lonely, which is why parents naturally gravitate to cuddling their children. As society has become more isolated, humans have moved away from casual touch. Many teachers balk at the idea of touching their students because they fear legal action, and even foster parents have expressed concerns about hugging the children they care for because they also worry they will be accused of wrongdoing. The cultural taboo against casual touch has become so strong that an entire industry has been invented to counteract the loneliness and touch deprivation that some people feel. In the United States and other countries, people can visit a cuddling workshop, where trained cuddlers will caress them and touch them gently for a specified period of time. Researchers told *The Guardian* that unless people can fight the stigma associated with casual touch, isolation and loneliness will likely become even more widespread, which could lead to an increase in stress-related disease in the general population.

Key Insight 5

Material possessions and personal accolades may provide a temporary mood boost, but won't lead to lasting happiness.

Analysis

In the 1990s, psychologist Tim Kasser began researching whether people who crave increased wealth are measurably happier than those who value spending time with friends or family. He studied hundreds of students, and discovered that those who covet fancy items or increased status had higher rates of depression. True happiness, Kasser learned, comes from pursuing enjoyable hobbies or forging deeper relationships, not from accruing more money or material goods.

Kasser was not the first to suggest that wealth doesn't lead to happiness; philosophers and religious leaders have been saying the same for thousands of years. In Buddhism, for example, practitioners are taught that suffering stems in part from the pursuit of material possessions. Wanting more wealth or fancy objects, under Buddhism's philosophy, never leads to permanent satisfaction, but only creates an increasingly insatiable lust for more. Buddhism warns its adherents that desiring wealth or status can only lead to more suffering and heartache. Seeking out happiness, likewise, is advised against, because earthly temptations only provide joy for a small period of time. In Christianity, practitioners are similarly warned against senseless greed. In a famous passage in the Bible, Jesus instructs a rich man to give up his possessions, and tells his followers that the wealthy will have a difficult time entering heaven because they cling to material possessions. Even though humans have known for centuries that wealth does not lead to happiness, it continues to be a source of frustration, stress, and envy, likely because the lack of it comes with its own set of problems.

Key Insight 6

Spending time in nature can decrease depression and anxiety.

Analysis

Living in a city without many green spaces likely will become depressing over time. Even someone who lives in a city with numerous parks is better off than someone who lives in an urban environment composed mostly of concrete and skyscrapers. Humans have an innate need to spend time around nature, and will mentally suffer if they experience prolonged isolation from natural environments.

Since a growing number of people are removed from natural environments, some researchers are attempting to create virtual avenues that reproduce the restorative effects of the outdoors. Author Florence Williams, while working on a book about the effects of nature on humans, visited Deltcho Valtchanov, a Canadian researcher at the University of Waterloo who created a computer-generated outdoor environment. Valtchanov used a program to measure whether virtual experiences produce physical and neurological responses similar to those experienced in real-world situations. Williams, however, was not impressed by Valtchanov's creation. While the deserted island she virtually visited was filled with beautiful plants, animal sounds, and other realistic visuals, it didn't feel like a real outdoor environment to her, and caused her to experience dizziness. At the end of her virtual tour, Valtchanov explained that Williams was not alone in preferring real nature to virtual worlds. More than a quarter of the test subjects for his virtual environment experienced dizziness and nausea, and in some cases needed to stop the experiment to avoid vomiting. Virtual reality may one day allow humans to explore nature without actually going outside, but for now it's a poor substitute for the real experience.

Key Insight 7

To decrease depression, sufferers must focus on something greater than themselves.

Analysis

In 2011, a group of impoverished people living in Berlin, Germany, rallied around an old Tunisian immigrant who had threatened to kill herself if she was evicted from her home. Developers had recently become interested in the area, and rent had gone up so much that long-term residents could no longer afford the area. The neighborhood's occupants had never spent time around each other before; the community was diverse and many were suspicious of those who held different values. However, by banding together to fight the rent hikes, community members gradually found ways to help each other solve personal problems, and depression rates in the neighborhood plummeted.

Caring for other humans is not the only way to mitigate self-interest and decrease levels of depression. Animal husbandry can provide some of the same benefits by giving caretakers a sense of responsibility and helping them develop an emotional bond with another living creature. A

2017 Reuters article explores a prison program in Maricopa County, Arizona, that allows inmates to take care of abused and neglected pets rescued from irresponsible owners. The women in the program are taken to an animal shelter six days a week to work with dogs, cats, and horses that have become antisocial because of mistreatment. As the animals start to warm up to human companionship again, they are adopted out to new owners. Inmates who participate in the program told Reuters that nurturing the abused animals gives them something to look forward to during their incarceration. Taking care of the animals not only helps the women boost their mood, but also helps them develop new skills that may become useful once they are released. By giving the women a chance to love and care for the pets that come through the animal shelter, both the prisoners and the animals are given a chance at rehabilitation, improving their chances of reintegrating with society at a later date.

Key Insight 8

If a community reduces social inequality and poverty, the rates of depression and anxiety will also decrease.

Analysis

In the 1970s, a town in Manitoba, Canada, underwent a novel experiment. Citizens were each promised a baseline annual income that would ensure that residents had enough money for food and shelter, regardless of whether they were able to retain their current jobs. Decades later, University of Manitoba researcher Evelyn Forget analyzed the data from the study and realized that not only did the program serve as an economic boon for the town, it also decreased the number of residents who needed to seek treatment for depression or anxiety.

Workplace insecurity, especially in the manufacturing sector, has made universal basic income an attractive idea for a growing number of people. A 2017 Gallup poll of more than 3,000 adults found that nearly half of US residents are in favor of providing universal basic income to workers whose jobs are eliminated by technology or automation. Among those who support such a program, the majority agree that the companies responsible for displacing those jobs should pay higher taxes to fund the universal basic income checks. Since the Gallup poll was based on a hypothetical proposal, it's unclear how much such a program would cost, or exactly how many workers in the United States would benefit. However, Gallup argues that nearly half of positions available in the United States could be replaced by technology eventually, meaning those workers will either have to find a new field, or will be out of a job altogether. Since universal basic income is hardly a reality across the nation in 2018, remaining manufacturing workers will still have to rely on their savings and their ability to adapt to new industries to survive. Those challenges will undoubtedly spark additional stress and worry among those who work in that sector, which may increase demand for mental health professionals who can care for their needs.

Important People

Johann Hari is a British journalist who has previously written for *The New York Times*, *The Guardian,* and *The New Republic*. His earlier work, *Chasing the Scream: The First and Last Days of the War on Drugs* (2015), was a *New York Times* bestseller.

John Haygarth (1740-1827) was a British physician who discovered the placebo effect.

George Brown is an anthropologist who interviewed a number of women with depression in London. He and **Tirril Harris** studied why the women were depressed and concluded their mood disorder was caused by negative life events.

Irving Kirsch is a Harvard Medical School professor who has studied the role of the placebo effect in antidepressants.

Tim Kasser is an American psychologist who studies the effect of materialism on mental health.

Evelyn Forget is a Canadian economist and professor who showed that universal basic income positively impacts a community's economy and the mental health of its residents.

Author's Style

Society's understanding of depression and anxiety has been slowly evolving for more than 50 years, and has required the combined efforts of scientists, mental health professionals, anthropologists, and everyday people. In *Lost Connections*, Johann Hari endeavors to include these multiple perspectives, providing readers with a multifaceted look at the common mood disorders that includes the experiences of patients and practitioners in Europe, Asia, and North America.

Hari doesn't only include perspectives from modern day experts and historical figures who made strides in the field of mental health. He also weaves in anecdotes from his own life, explaining his struggles with depression and how he turned to antidepressants to solve the overwhelming sadness that began haunting him as a teenager. His personal stories often provide a respite for readers who may feel overwhelmed by the broad number of scientific studies that Hari includes, and demonstrate that Hari understands how frustrating fighting depression can be.

Lost Connections, which is divided into three parts, first explores research conducted into depression between the early twentieth century and the 2010s. Hari then examines nine social, psychological, and physical causes of depression, before moving on to seven methods that society could implement to help people reduce their depression and reconnect with each other. The book has 22 chapters, as well as a prologue, introduction, and conclusion. Hari additionally includes a notes section which provides further information about his sources.

Author's Perspective

For decades, Johann Hari believed what his doctors told him: that his depression was caused by a chemical imbalance in his brain. When he began looking into the science behind depression and anxiety, he realized that story was not only simplified — it was harmful. *Lost Connections* provides a more nuanced look at the societal, psychological, and mental forces that cause depression and anxiety, as well as the cultural changes needed to reverse the growing trend of mood disorders in a number of developed nations.

Although much of Hari's book looks at depression and anxiety from an academic and journalistic standpoint, he makes clear that the topic is still deeply personal. After learning that antidepressants likely don't have a noticeable, long-lasting effect on depression, Hari wrestles with his own dismay and anger. He repeatedly uses his own emotional reactions to prepare readers for information that might be difficult to digest, and encourages skeptics to dig into the research he explores in his work.

In one part of *Lost Connections*, Hari briefly alludes to allegations he once faced regarding his journalistic integrity. Hari was accused of plagiarism because he presented quotes from experts as if they were said directly to him, when in fact he was using statements made to other journalists without attribution. He admitted to the charges in a 2018 interview with *The Guardian*, and stated that he was wrong to misrepresent the source of the quotes. His actions cost him a columnist position at the British publication *The Independent*.

Hari does not view *Lost Connections* as a guidebook that depressed readers can use to seek personal recovery, but rather as an in-depth investigation that shows how humans could collectively fight depression and anxiety. He argues that forging deeper connections with each other, and resisting the urge to isolate or over-medicalize a person's reaction, is essential to that goal. Individual attempts to alleviate mood disorders, either through pills or self-improvement, will likely fail because they don't address the person's innate need for companionship and community.

Printed in Great Britain
by Amazon